UNLOCKED

KEYS TO GETTING OUT
AND STAYING OUT

CHANCE A. JOHNMEYER

DEDICATION

I dedicate this book to my wife Reni, who has been by my side loyally for the last 22 years. In some sense she has walked the beat with me, listening as I shared with her my moments of triumph and my walk thru the darkness of the human soul. She was, and remains, the light at the end of shift. If it weren't for her I would not have stayed.

TABLE OF CONTENTS

FOREWORD

When an author works to get an understanding into the soul of another, they often pass on to another unintended recipient a sense of their own soul. In his unveiled attempt to understand and empathize with "Troy" and others in similar circumstances, the author has passed on to me a look into my own soul, and an attempt to understand the legacy my parents passed on to me. Something I have never been led to discover before!

It is my sincere hope that each of you who read this book find this also for yourself.

In reaching an understanding of even only one (1) human being, there is a better understanding of one's own self-worth and the desire of all human beings to be remembered.

Every life has a "story." That "story" lasts only as long as the last person who tells it. What's your story?

Felice Enright
Author

INTRODUCTION

They say a prison officer is down fifty percent of the time he has worked, so for me that is a seven year bid. I came to prison as a young officer in January of 2001, walking thru the front door of New Hampshire State Prison for Men in Concord. I had left a hot, dusty job as a factory worker making guns for Sturm, Ruger & Co. At the time, my peers said I would never make it six months, yet here I am fourteen years later writing to you.

It was here behind the concrete and barbed wire that I began to be challenged about everything that I thought I knew, about humanity, about the soul. It was here that I came face to face with the reality of so many people— Prison! The prison experience is unlike anything I have ever experienced. It began, and continues, to transform who I am and how I respond to people in my life .

At the end of 2006 my advanced education in humanity would continue as my family and I closed the NH chapter and moved south below the Mason Dixon Line to Florida. Florida was a totally different animal altogether; it seemed caught in a time warp, hesitant to change. The old south elements of prison operations were still deeply rooted, but still in a lot of ways it was the same as up north.

I watched men of all races leave the gates after serving their time—excited, with dreams and ambitions, going out to retake their lives. Some would never return; others within a short time would be back in the yard, with their heads hanging down, a sense of failure. They had been beaten by poor choices and consequences. These, combined with an unreasonable criminal justice system, made it seem like a losing battle for them as they tried to reenter society.

I've seen, and continue to see, a lot of guys coming back. It has always bothered me, to see a man return, with pain in his eyes. I continue to ask *why?* This book attempts to answer that question.

You will find within these pages mental notes and life lessons, written, erased, and rewritten again after years of walking the upper deck, standing cell front, and watching the yard. I have gained much insight by talking and asking questions, listening as grown men broke down their lives in front of me from beginning to the end.

The truth has always been my cause; for an officer, or an inmate, it didn't matter. I would seek it out aggressively, like a detective uncovering the lies. My hope is that you find in my writings truth and understanding. My hope is that what I have presented challenges you to the deepest part of your soul.

You will meet Troy, an inmate that worked for me in 2014, as he details out his thoughts with only 30 days left to go. Troy was on a different path, constantly reading and taking notes, working to take what he had learned and use it to change what was going on inside his head. While everybody else was eating everything that wasn't nailed down or challenging each other on how many push-ups they could do, Troy was working out his mind. It's for the "Troy's" that I write this book.

Included you will find dozens of pages of carefully selected resources for Florida residents, all the real-world practical information that I have seen inmates struggle to find. I believe information empowers people, giving them the confidence to succeed.

This section includes information on:
- Federal Bonding
- Guidelines for those incarcerated, by Federal Student Aid
- Contact information for top schools for cooking, welding, HVAC, and solar
- Child support modification forms and more practical information to assist in your transition

You and I both know, everything is not black and white or cut and dry. This book will not claim to have all the answers, nor will I tell you, "If you do X, Y, or Z, this will happen." What I will tell you is, *"If you take what you find here, think over it, and put it into practice, it will help you to stand free, and just maybe you will never… circle back around to be in this dark place again."*

CHAPTER ONE
TROY

Where did all the time go? It just seems like yesterday that I got here… Truth be told, I haven't made any positive use of my time while I've been down. All in all I didn't do the time. I let the time do me. I have all these tattoos, twice convicted felon, and flat on my ass when I get out. What the hell am I even getting out for? At least in here I have three hot's and a cot! Out there ain't nothin given to nobody. My family abandoned me long ago, my friends showed me their true colors the minute I stepped foot in here, and my girl… Let's not even go there. It all happened so fast, and now shit's fixin' to get real.

When I first started this bid I couldn't even see this far down the road. Looking back, it didn't matter anyway, everything was a blur. Today though, thinking about the day they let me out that gate… That is clear as day. I'm not really any different now, than when I stepped out of that van in chains, ten years ago.

Now that I am face to face with the future, the time I have done doesn't seem all that bad. What sucks though is the thought of starting all over from scratch. I've been out once before. When I got out, I really thought I was gunna make it. I went back to where I grew up, tried to find a job, and get settled in. Everybody I ran into, who knew me from before, they half-way listened, talking to me, while lookin' at someone else. They weren't really listenin'. I tried to tell them I was a changed man, but it didn't matter.

You know this is depressing. I sometimes think "The System" is designed specifically for me to fail. I feel like the boot is against my neck, and I can't move.

I'm not looking for handouts, just something different, and anything to keep me from coming back to the chain gang.

If I don't find anything, I'm gunna do what I got to do. I refuse to go around not having anything. I just hope I don't get caught again. If I do, they ain't letting me out, and I ain't havin' that.

CHAPTER TWO
WHAT'S ON YA MIND

"That's real." Do you connect with this guy? The writings of Troy are blood raw, and as I get older I come to appreciate that approach more, over some mask of nice words.

Like Troy, this is not the first time for many of you. You've gotten out before and made an honest run at it, but somehow the cards didn't seem to fall in your favor, and you had to fold. The streets were like an evil seductress, calling you to her pleasures, fulfilling your greatest desires. You soon learned she's never happy, she always wants more, and you chase after her spending your all, until you're bankrupt and have nothing left to give.

Since you've been down, your friends have left, and you dread seeing the chaplain, afraid he will call your name and let you know someone close has passed away—and you couldn't be there. Your kids are all grown up, and they barely know you. But it seems that God, if you believe in him, has smiled upon you, and you get another chance at life. You're getting out. Once again you will breathe in fresh air and experience sweet freedom. Soon you will open your eyes to someone you love sleeping peacefully beside you, not to the lights being turned on at an ungodly hour by a burned out CO with an attitude calling *"Count!"*

When you hear that last "buzz" to the outside gate, it will all change... Or will it? Are you ready?

During my time as an officer, I have walked rounds, hundreds of them, talking with guys just like you, desperate for conversation, something meaningful, different than the day in and day out nonsense.

I have come to realize thru all of these conversations that those who come to prison and return to prison are those who struggle in 5 main areas.

The command center for these five areas begins with *"What's on Ya Mind"*: your thoughts.

> "Be careful of your thoughts, for your thoughts become your words. Be careful of your words, for your words become your actions. Be careful of your actions, for your actions become your habits. Be careful of your habits, for your habits become your character. Be careful of your character, for your character becomes your destiny."
>
> — *Chinese proverb, author unknown*

"We can't escape pain; we can't escape the essential nature of our lives. But we do have a choice. We can give in and relent, or we can fight, persevere, and create a life worth living, a noble life. Pain is a fact; our evaluation of it is a choice."

— Jacob Held
See more at:
http://www.movemequotes.com/top-15-power-of-positive-thinking-quotes/#sthash.5dNUZJgB.dpuf

THOUGHTS ARE POWERFUL

I remember one time in 2006 when I was the commanding officer in the SHU unit. This inmate, I forget his name, requested use of the hair clippers. I told him I would talk to the sarge and get back with him. We were busy caring for the remaining 80 to 100 inmates, and we were unable to fulfill his request within the time frame he thought it should be done. Several rounds later, I stopped to speak with him, and I stared in disbelief. He had pulled just about every strand of hair from his head with just his fingertips. His response: "Now I look like a dumbass, and I have visits this weekend." I couldn't help but chuckle: a sprig of hair here, a sprig of hair there. I was taken aback by the extreme measures this individual was willing to take to accomplish his desires.

In that cell by himself, with no opposing views, he began to focus on negative thoughts and perceived injustices. His thoughts became his reality.

At times we get alone and our brain gets stuck on rewind and replay. We become convinced that our thoughts are our reality. Those thoughts, when allowed to run wild, can become our puppet master.

While researching for this book I came across this from marriage and family therapist Robert C. Jameson: "What we think often comes out of our mouth and into someone else's ears. Our words impact how we feel about ourselves and they can impact how others think and feel.

"Words are symbols that communicate what's going on inside our head to us and others. We share our fears, our sorrow, our joy, our love and our dreams with our words.

"Our words create action. Our words can create intimacy or separation. With our words we can motivate ourselves to do things we never thought we could do, and our words can also move others to step forward into their own personal power so they can be of service to their community. Words can calm us or excite us. Words can actually change the direction of a nation. So watch what you think and be aware of the words that come from your thoughts, and the actions that follow your words."

In other words, in "How to Control Your Mind and Thoughts," Buddhist monk Mathieu Ricard said, "Thoughts can be our best friends and our worst enemies."

Being incarcerated takes a toll on the human body without the previous daily physical activity of working and weekend recreation. So a lot of inmates work out like crazy. The brain, like the body, needs to be worked out by putting into practice the following:

MEDITATE DAILY

If you're one of those people who quickly excuses yourself as having tried meditation and discovering it did not work for you, that's the first thought you need to change. Why? Because it isn't so. What does it mean to meditate? According to Dictionary.com it means nothing more than *"to engage in thought or contemplation; reflect."*

We all meditate. We just need to decide what we reflect ("meditate") on, or what we value. Sitting on your bunk fantasizing as you read the pages of the latest urban book, or dreaming about cartels, is probably not profitable for a successful future. Instead, it builds thinking that is wrong and deceitful. It strengthens already destructive thinking. The most deceived person is one-and-the-same with the deceiver.

You *can* learn to meditate, and you must, if you wish to learn to control your thoughts and your thinking.

OBSERVE YOUR THOUGHTS

We all have negative thoughts. In his book *The Happiness Trap*, author Russ Harris says 80% of everyone's thoughts contain some sort of negative content. So it's normal to have negative thoughts. The Christian's "Jesus," who was in all points "tempted" as we are yet WITHOUT sin, had negative thoughts. This understanding changed me forever, because I was always beating myself up because my thoughts were not always perfect.

Late one night I was working in the control room perched high above the walls at NH State Prison. In a quiet moment, I looked over the compound and realized that, in a very real way, the one called Jesus had the same thoughts as every man I was watching over, yet he did no wrong. Wow!

The first nanosecond of a moment, the "seed thought," or temptation is neither right nor wrong. They just are. Don't judge them; rather, observe their beginning. What gave birth to them? Where were you when the thought first occurred?

How many times has a thought popped into your mind—let's say some kind of judgmental thought such as anger, jealousy, or vengeance about a cell mate or an officer, and instantly, *bam!* We jump into judgment mode, finding fault with others or ourselves, thinking something negative. It's how you respond to your "seed" thought that introduces the "rightness" or "wrongness" of them. How many times have you or someone you know ended up in the box because they shot their mouth off without first thinking? Consequences are a great teacher.

When you get out, your mind will be flooded with thoughts good and bad *"Man, I am out, I am free!"* Or, *"That b*#ch is not going to talk to me like that!"*

"I have been out here for two weeks trying to find work, and still nothing."

"Hey man, I see ya struggling! I'm gunna help ya out. Just make this delivery for me, and I'll take care of ya."

Those of you reading this book right now that have been involved in the sale of narcotics, you will be tempted to sell again, numerous times.

To go mentally from making stupid money to working for a working man's wage requires a complete restructuring of your mind.

Husbands and wives, you will be faced by a spouse who has managed the affairs of the family while you were locked down, and all of a sudden you get home and a second opinion will not be heard easily. Service families go through these challenges all the time when one spouse or another returns home from service overseas.

Oftentimes in the heat of the moment things are said that hurt and enrage. Once you shoot your mouth off and let those words fly, there's no taking them back, and they land like a hatchet. When you observe these potentially destructive, life-changing thoughts, you must deal with them! Failure to do so will cause poison to come out of your mouth, wounding those closest to you, your spouse, your children, your mom, your dad. These words create deep, deep pain. Left unchecked, unforgiveness will begin to take root and overshadow your future legacy.

Listed below are some mental tools to consider using when confronted with unprofitable thoughts:

CAST THEM DOWN

All thoughts pass through the observation stage.

When you get out and have little to nothing, it isn't fun.

The temptation of easy money is everywhere. I mean money makes the world go 'round, right? So make some quick money by whatever means, go to the store, buy some new clothes, and then investigate the pleasures of the first person that comes along, and you're straight, right? If you choose the path just mentioned, you are not driven by wisdom, logic, or reason, but by impulse. Impulse doesn't think about where it's been, or where it's going; its only concern is the here and now.

You have two choices; you can water these thoughts by spending time meditating on them, or you can cast them down refusing to let it rent space in your head.

Meditation is like watering a plant, growing what is meditated on, good or evil! You can meditate on evil, and it will grow and take over your life, or you can starve it. In other words, in the purported words of Martin Luther, "You cannot keep a bird from flying over your head; what you can do is prevent it from building a nest in your hair."

REPLACE THEM

When destructive thoughts show up, we must begin to discipline ourselves to redirect our mind, replacing thoughts of failure with success. Ex-Navy Seal Cade Courtley, currently a survival specialist, details how the US military uses visualization techniques to practice what they call emergency conditioning (EC). It means conditioning the mind in advance of emergencies, thus producing psychological strength in times of crisis. This is also referred to as "battle-proofing" or "battle inoculation" by military personnel. Example: A soldier lying on his cot imagines a nasty firefight with the enemy, including what it will sound like and smell like, the heavy breathing, and the utter exhaustion.

If the brain imagines something in deep and vivid detail, it will become part of a person's "experience files."

This visualization exercise will actually fool the brain into believing that you have already experienced this event. You can tap into these files at will by hitting the play button that starts the "movie" of what you have already visualized and planned. It will seem more or less familiar if ever you are confronted with a similar experience. (Courtley)

You may choose to reflect on those you love, your mother, your children, your girl, or even friends and family. Reflect on times spent together at church, sports events, parties, and times like that, and hold them in place by playing out that memory in your mind. These are times that you're thankful for. They enrich our lives.

In the short term try a "gratitude journal," a term created by Robert A. Emmons of the University of California, Davis, a technique used in his pioneering experiment conducted with Michael E. McCullough of the University of Miami.

They instructed people to keep a journal listing five things for which they felt grateful, like a friend's generosity, something they'd learned, or a sunset they'd enjoyed.

The gratitude journal was brief—just one sentence for each of the five things—and done only once a week, but after two months there were significant effects.

Compared with a control group, the people keeping the gratitude journal were more optimistic and felt happier. They reported fewer physical problems and spent more time working out. This is a great idea, because some of us have spent our lives focusing on the negative.

Maybe it began with our parents being overly critical, so we began looking inward, focusing on our mistakes, trying to do better to escape their criticism. As we grew older our focus went to others and their mistakes, as a defense mechanism to help us feel better about ourselves. The journal is a plausible way to begin to retrain the mind. We have to purpose to see positive, good things. Once we see those good things happening to us and write them down, we begin to visualize in a very concrete way the good that is happening to us. Some of you may even carry the journal further into the future.

In some circumstances I have chosen to begin singing. As crazy as it sounds, we all have memories of songs we learned as a child, and as we make an active decision to begin singing those songs or other good songs, our thought processes begin to shift away from the negative thoughts and impulses.

You might be saying, *"This dude is crazy. I am not about to start singing some crazyass children's songs."*

I say to you, *"Cool. The way you've been doing things, how's that working for ya"?*

What researchers are beginning to discover is that singing is like an infusion of the perfect tranquilizer, the kind that both soothes your nerves and elevates your spirits.

The elation may come from endorphins, a hormone released by singing, which is associated with feelings of pleasure. Or it might be from oxytocin, another hormone released during singing, which has been found to alleviate anxiety and stress. Oxytocin also enhances feelings of trust and bonding, which may explain why still more studies have found that singing lessens feelings of depression and loneliness. The benefits of singing regularly seem to be cumulative.

In one study, singers, especially choir singers, were found to have lower levels of cortisol, indicating lower stress.

Do you still believe singing is stupid? Sing!

OVERWHELM THEM

Sometimes you will experience thoughts that are evil and stubborn, and as hard as you try, you just can't cast them down or replace them. Maybe you have given thought to them for too long, and now they seem overwhelming. If you truly desire success you're going to have to do some things differently. In situations like these, physical activities that exhaust the body also overwhelm thoughts. When you make an active decision to hit the gym, practice martial arts, or go biking, your body often times will begin to talk louder than your thoughts. Combine this with music or a source of different information, such sports or news radio that is positive by nature, it will counter what you are thinking. Turn it on and turn it up, and begin to refocus your mind towards your success.

CULTIVATE THE SPACE BETWEEN THOUGHTS

In other words, as you train yourself to be the observer of your mind andyour thoughts, you are actually cultivating what easterners call "the primary consciousness" that underlies all thinking. It is that *"space between the notes,"* said Claude Debussy *"that makes the music."*

What does it mean to cultivate? I grew up in Missouri on a 600 acre farm. My family grew what we called row crops. This included things like corn, soybeans, and wheat. Several months after everything had been planted my dad would have to go thru with a cultivator. It was a large piece of machinery hooked behind a tractor that was spaced so as not to destroy the plants. This cultivator would dig deep, breaking up the stony ground and allowing rain and air into the soil and digging up the weeds. We, like the cultivator, must keep the ground stirred up by practices that keep us challenged.

Things like reading challenge the mind. I read everything. When we take in positive information that reinforces life and success, challenging adversity and succeeding, we keep the mind fresh. We keep it stirred up. What we take in is in essence the space between the notes.

> *"A man's mind may be likened to a garden, which may be intelligently cultivated or allowed to run wild; but whether cultivated or neglected, it must, and will, bring forth. If no useful seeds are put into it, then an abundance of useless weed seeds will fall therein, and will continue to produce their kind."*
>
> *—James Allen, As a Man Thinketh*

If there were no spaces, no "stirring up" between the notes, "your decisions" on the sheet music of "your life" would seem unintelligible, meaningless, and maybe even annoying. This space is the place of internal peace. It is what some call "pure consciousness." It will influence how decisions are made.

Cast Down, Replace, Overwhelm, and Cultivate: four mental practices to help gain control of your thoughts.

CHAPTER THREE
FOOL'S GOLD

"For where your treasure is, there will your heart be also."

— *Luke 12:34*

Once your feet hit the bricks, it's back to the grind, the struggle, the hustle! How you grind, struggle, or hustle is determined by what you value, and what you value is what you put your heart into.

What you value, you will sacrifice to get! What are you willing to sacrifice? Is it creating a strong foundation for your kids, by promoting a strong family, education, and morals? Are you willing to sacrifice that? Sometimes as men it is hard to keep our priorities straight and balanced. We're tempted to put money and its accumulation above family, above teaching our children the value of morals such as integrity and respect. When we lose sight of these, when we lose balance, we lose out, those closest to us suffer, and things begin to spiral out of control.

Let me ask you a question. What did you value the most when you were on the outside, Money, power, or pleasure? R&B Artist Usher has a new 2015 song, something about ho's, and Shawty dancing on poles, and… money. You get the point.

Not a bad song, right? You know how it is, handling yo biz, it's just another form of hustle, right? Now replace Shawty with your daughter's name. No? Can you see now how changing the thought process changes the value? We see in Usher's lyrics what he values. "Money!"

I was talking with this inmate known as Zoe about this song one day, and he got mad at me, because he likes Usher. "You have it all wrong," he replied. "You're focusing on the hook. What Usher is trying to say is that it doesn't matter how you get your money, I will still love you." I understand that for many in our culture, this has become the new "Real.".. But look! The value of money is redefining the boundaries of right and wrong, and the methods used to obtain it. How many children have had mothers and fathers who have chosen to chase after quick money and gotten busted in their choices, and now instead of raising their children and encouraging them through the tough years to get their education and build their identity, those parents are in prison. Their children are left to their own impulses, sometimes with no loving direction. Is it any wonder that our little girls are ending up in seedy strip clubs with dishonorable men looking upon them?

When you were kicking it in the street, what did you spend the majority of your time doing? What rules did you play by while you were hustlin'" "The Code"? It's all about getting paid, right, no snitching? How is your street investment serving you now? Never mind the guy that is sleeping next to you with a couple K in his canteen. How is *your* investment serving you right *now*? "The Code" is a liar and a thief stealing sons and daughters, moms and dads. I have lost count of the number of conversations I've had where parents are no longer talking to their sons or daughters. They're not sending canteen money or letters. How many mothers have stripped a father's children away from him because he has sworn an unwritten allegiance to the code of the street? It is an enemy; stop treating it like it deserves some kind of honor. It doesn't. It has robbed your past and your present. Will it also rob you of your future? We are all guilty of treasuring the wrong things. The things that we treasure, the things that we find valuable, are the things that we chase after. Will it be money, pleasure, possessions? We spend time maintaining this and polishing that, struggling to get more. We think just a little bit more, or a newer one, will make our life better, but is that the case?

In the following sections name three things that you chased after when you were free. Be honest, good or bad, and then follow that with the consequences or reward. Did you give up anything in exchange for it?

1.)

2.)

3.)

What do you value now? Sitting down with your family during visits, your niece, daughter, son, or nephew? How many of you have had a small child fall asleep in your lap because they felt safe? These are things that money can't buy, power blinds to, and prestige doesn't care about.

Take a moment and list three things that you value now, and why it is important to value these things:

1.)

2.)

3.)

What are your thoughts about the exercise above? Did you find that maybe the things you once valued really weren't all that valuable? Has your value system begun to change?

When we value good and chase after good one day at a time, it strengthens us through accomplishment, making us, our children, our marriage, and our communities stronger. It helps to encourage us for the next moment. The things we value the most are what we put our heart and soul into. As we get ready to leave, check yourself. Are you digging for "real" or just "Fool's Gold"?

CHAPTER FOUR
KRYPTONITE

"Fear makes the wolf bigger than he is."

— German Proverb

As children we were all familiar with Superman and the power Kryptonite had over him. When he came in contact with it, it would take away his powers to resist evil, and he could barely move.

Inside the fence, in our world, fear is "kryptonite" It takes away our true identity, our power to stand up for ourselves. It forces us to adapt, or to be "put down." So we pretend "fear" doesn't exist; it's for women, sissies, or the weak. We make ourselves appear "hard," absent of any appearance of fear.

Probably one of the greatest stumbling stones to getting back on your feet out on the streets is the stone of fear hanging around your neck, dragging you down. Troy had fears, remember…

"I have all these tattoos, twice convicted felon."

— *Fear of Perception*

Wrong perception has been around since the dawn of time. In the 2004 drama film *Crash*, director Paul Haggis did an amazing job smashing stereotypes. Cast member Michael Pena played Daniel Ruiz, a locksmith and ex-con out on the street, just trying to play by the rules and take care of his daughter.

I remember when he was first shown on the movie screen. He had tattoos up the side of his neck. I remember thinking, "Yeh! You see those tattoos, that's a gang member."

Yep, that was me, the stereotypical CO judging people. That movie wrecked me. The director sucked me in to a scene, set me up with my prejudices, and then smashed me into the wall with facts that were counter to the prejudice I had created in my mind.

Perception is changed by challenging prejudices. You are not your tattoos! Grab any opportunity that comes your way and prove the naysayers wrong. Do it once! Do it a thousand times!

"What the hell am I even getting out for?"

— *Fear of Purpose*

Without purpose it's almost impossible to determine direction. If you don't know where you're going, it's so easy to not do anything. You become motionless. You end up back at the beginning trying to figure out your purpose, and it's in these moments that we begin to question our value. That's where the quote from Lewis Carrol comes in, *"If you don't know where you are going, any road will get you there."*

Do something take any road, just move! Reach out, ask for help up and help out. This is especially important if you're a parent. Your children are watching you and learning how to respond to adversity.

"Whether you think you can, or think you can't, you will."

— *Henry Ford, Founder of Ford Motor Company*

"My family abandoned me long ago."

— *Fear of Being Alone*

This is probably one of the most painful. Now after being incarcerated for a period of time, you realize the abandonment by your family is partially your fault. You have to acknowledge that and take responsibility for it, without conditions. When you return, a few kind acts may not repair a lifetime of rejecting their advice. You must purpose to restore relationships with your family. It's not the fear of being alone that terrifies you, but the fear of the abandonment lasting forever.

"What sucks is the thought of starting all over from scratch."

— *Fear of Starting Over*

I was talking with this young inmate the other day; let's call him Sherif. I had noticed as the day wore on that his usual demeanor was different, so I went to talk to him. "What's on your mind, man?" He replied that he was thinking about his sorrows. I asked him, "What are your sorrows? He told me "his fears"—things like poverty, fear of leaving the old life, and losing his youth. He understood what he was facing and he showed a level of maturity far beyond his years. I was impressed by his wisdom.

Starting over requires leaving the old life. I hadn't really thought much about leaving the old life until then. As I began to think through that, I came to realize that he and I weren't all that different. When we grow accustomed to a certain way of life for a period of time, it's familiar and safe. We understand the boundaries, the rules, and the risk. It's when we are challenged to step out of that life into something else that fear begins to invade. That's when you begin to seek compromise in your mind. You begin to ponder what it might look like when you get out. *"Maybe I can go back and just take out the things that led up to me coming to prison?"* But there is one problem: The old friends still have their addictions, and their love for the fast life… They haven't grown up.

PRACTICAL KEYS FOR DEALING WITH FEAR

You might be saying to yourself, *"Okay, Chance, I get it! You wanted me to admit that fear is a part of my life. It is. I'm scared to death! What can I do, so that these fears will let me go?"*

- Talk about feelings and fears that you or family members may have. It's OK to feel sad and frustrated. Being sad is not a sickness; it's a normal human emotion

- Decide together with your family or caregiver what things you can do to support each other.

- Do not blame yourself or others when you feel anxious and afraid. Instead, look at your thoughts, concerns, and beliefs related to what has been going on in your life.

- Get help through in-person or online support groups.
- Think about asking your doctor or nurse for a referral to a counselor or mental health professional who can work with you and your family.
- Use prayer, meditation, or other types of spiritual support.
- Try deep breathing and relaxation exercises several times a day. (For example, close your eyes, breathe deeply, focus on each body part, and relax it, starting with your toes and working up to your head. When you're relaxed, imagine yourself in a pleasant place, such as a breezy beach or a sunny meadow.)
- Cut down on caffeine and stay away from alcohol; they can worsen anxiety symptoms.
- Talk with your doctor about the possible use of medicine for anxiety.

The practical keys mentioned above are solid and will help you deal with thoughts of fear that may have you pinned down, or are telling you to just give up. The same principles that we talked about in Chapter 1 also apply to our fears.

Cast Down the fear that overcomes you. Chances are the thoughts that you fear the most haven't even happened.

Replace the thoughts of fear with thoughts of faith and confidence. There are some things we can control and other things we cannot; cast the ones you can't control on faith, or they will own you and become your master.

Overwhelm thoughts of fear and failure. Don't stay where you're having thoughts of fear; get out of your dark house or apartment, turn on the radio, jump out of plane, do something! Cultivate thoughts of success and imagine yourself pushing through your fears to the point that it no longer holds control over you.

CHAPTER FIVE
LET IT GO

Prison has to be the biggest test to loyalty I've ever seen. Troy felt it, I've seen it. You know what I'm talking about. Those friends that went with you everywhere on the street, your girl that says she'll ride with you to the end, and parents, that's a given, right? I mean, they're blood, right?

When you first came to prison everything starts off pretty good considering the circumstances. When you can catch a turn on the phones and you hear the voices of the ones you love, it brings a smile to your face. *"Everything is going to be alright, babe!"* Some of you start off getting a letter every day, with perfume on the pages, driving you crazy with promises of undying love. You think, *"I'm going to be okay; I'm going to make it."*

Then as time drags on the letters begin to slow down; you anxiously wait as the CO thumbs through to the last letter, waiting to hear your name called. No longer are they coming once a day, but once a week, and you're lying in your bunk sweating to death, staring at the ceiling fan and wondering, "Is she going to stay with me to the end? Who is that b*#ch with?" For some of you, your parents started by sending money in to your canteen, but they ended up missing a couple of payments, and now all of a sudden you have to shower with this small ass sliver of soap that the state gives you, expecting it to last for two weeks. You have to brush your teeth with some toothpaste that tastes like god knows what. For others, your mom and dad sent you nothing, not a dime, and still others have nobody.

These experiences are real for a lot of you in the jails and prisons all over the United States and the world. Your mind takes off and runs to pain. You feel a sense of betrayal, and you begin to feel... alone. Due to the routine of canteen and mail, you are forced to face your aloneness over and over. You face feelings of anger, and as anger takes root, those moments once sweet turn to bitterness. Bitterness can begin to infect everything in our day to day relationships. It's like a seed.

When I was a kid my dad's favorite pastime seemed to be making me work. We owned a large farm in central Missouri with lots of pasture for the cows to graze in. In between spring and summer the milk thistle plants would begin to blossom. If you didn't deal with them early, the beautiful purple flower at the top of the stem would begin to dry out. The hot summer winds would come along, causing the seeds to take flight, and they would plant themselves wherever they landed. My dad would take me out in the farm truck with a garden hoe in the blistering heat, and I had to dig out those thistles from the root. They were everywhere. Being a kid and hating work, I just wanted to get done, so I would sometimes just cut them off level at the ground. My dad would come back later to check on me, and he always found the ones I cut off at the ground and would make me go back and make sure the root was cut out. He would say, "Chance, if you don't get the root out, they will just come back next year." He was right. We came back one year, and they had almost taken over the field.

At first glance feelings of bitterness seem beneficial and beautiful, like the thistle—nice to look at from a distance. It makes you feel as if you are in control of your injustice. But as you probably know by now, it spreads and takes over everything, it is actually in control of you.

FIVE DARK "BENEFITS" OF UNFORGIVENESS

- **BENEFIT:** *Debt is power.* There is power in having something to hold over another's head. There is power in using a person's weakness and failure against him or her. In moments when we want our own way—let's say you need money put in your canteen, or you need a gambling debt paid off—it's amazing what we can remember in order to manipulate something in our favor. So we pull out some wrong against us as our relational trump card to manipulate. **CONSEQUENCE:** You devalue the other person. Those that feel as if they have no value in life struggle with understanding their purpose in this life, and you end up making that worse This can lead to a whole host of issues: depression, anger, and addictions.

- **BENEFIT:** *Debt is identity.* Holding onto another's sin, weakness, and failure can make you feel superior to them. It allows you to believe that you are more righteous and mature than they are. We fall into this pattern of getting our sense of self by comparing ourselves to others. You might say to yourself, *"I would never do anything like that!"* This pattern plays into the thoughts of self-righteousness that are common with every person. **CONSEQUENCE:** If someone comes along and seeks to resolves the injustice against you by apologizing or asking for your forgiveness, then you have nothing that sets you above them. You have nothing to compare your wrongs with, causing some of you to struggle with your own identity and value.

- **BENEFIT:** *Debt is entitlement.* Because of all the other person's wrongs against us, he or she owes us. Carrying these wrongs makes us feel deserving and therefore comfortable with being self-focused and demanding. "After all I deserve to respond this way. " **CONSEQUENCE:** In the process of collecting your debt through unforgiveness you risk the possibility of demanding more in repayment than the injustice requires. This can open a Pandora's Box of events in retaliation against you.

- **BENEFIT:** *Debt is weaponry.* The sins and failures that another has done against you become like a loaded gun that we carry around. In a moment's notice during a casual conversation, someone will challenge our thoughts and opinions. Our mind recalls hypocrisies and wrong doings committed against us by the one in question and we blast them, driving them back a safe distance. When someone has hurt us in some way, it is very tempting to hurt them back by throwing in their face just how evil and immature they are. **CONSEQUENCE:** You reach a point, especially when it comes to family, that you begin to realize you're the one holding the gun. You're doing the shooting, and after you have shot everybody with your bitterness and anger it begins to feel pointless to keep shooting them. You begin to realize exactly who it is you shot, and you begin to come down on yourself living a life of regret, never breaking free to achieve success. When we're constantly cutting people by reminding them of their wrongs, there comes a point when nobody wants to be around us anymore and we're all alone, expressed through multiple relationships and broken marriages.

- **BENEFIT:** *Debt puts us in the position of being god.* It is the one place that we must never be, but it is also a position that all of us have put ourselves in. We are not the judge of others. As tempting as it may be to exact your own punishment for a wrongdoing, it's not the right of anyone. We are not the one who should dispense consequences for other people's sins. It is not our job to make sure they feel the appropriate amount of guilt for what they have done. But it is very tempting to climb up and sit down on God's throne and to make ourselves judge. **CONSEQUENCE:** Playing God is expensive; exacting justice feels good in the moment, but it cost you freedom and relationships with those you love, your kids, your girlfriend, and your wife! Playing God in the moment can impact the future of all those closest to you far into the future.

So as you can see that while there are supposed "benefits" to unforgiveness, the benefits are small in comparison to the consequences, and those consequences last for years and multiple generations. So for the sake of your success, and the success of your children, you should do everything in your pwoer to prevent the seed thought of bitterness from taking root and becoming unforgiveness.

How should you respond to unforgiveness? How do you gain control over the thoughts that rule your emotions?

- Understand that forgiveness *is not* forgetting, nor does it mean condoning or excusing offenses! We all have had some bad life stories of different actions committed against us.

Some were committed by those closest to us, people who we placed our deepest trust in, like our mothers, our fathers, maybe even our wife or girlfriend. Though forgiveness can help repair a damaged relationship, it doesn't obligate you to reconcile with the person who harmed you, or release them from legal accountability.

Instead, forgiveness brings peace of mind and frees you from corrosive anger. While there is some debate over whether true forgiveness requires positive feelings toward the offender, experts agree that it at least involves letting go of deeply held negative feelings. In that way, it empowers you to recognize the pain you suffered without letting that pain define you, enabling you to heal and move on with your life.

- Understand that forgiveness is an action word and a process. For some it doesn't just happen. Forgiveness is making an active decision in the moment not to retaliate against someone for an injustice committed against you by talking down to them or reminding them of their past failures. Forgiveness is refusing to hold a grudge. Forgiveness is releasing them from your payback.

- Consider the definition of true love. After some research in the different religions of the world, I have concluded that while many of the different religions give broad generalizations about love, Christianity is the only belief that goes into great detail defining love. In the 1st book of Corinthians, love is defined as kind and patient, never jealous, boastful, proud, or rude. Love isn't selfish or quick tempered. It doesn't keep a record of wrongs that others do.

Love rejoices in the truth, but not in evil. Love is always supportive, loyal, hopeful, and trusting. Love never fails! You love your family, right? But if you go back a couple of sentences you see that true love "keeps no record of wrongdoings." Unforgiveness cannot exist in the spirit of true love—only forgiveness can.

- Live in the Present! If you're reading this, or if today is the day you're stepping out the gate, *"You're in the present!"* The energy you exert to go back in time is energy prepared for the present moment. Go back and read Chapter 1. When you find your mind going back into the past, revisiting past hurts, you must make an active decision in the present to change that by **Casting Down**, by **Replacing**, or by **Overcoming**. Your future success depends on it.

"You must live in the present, launch yourself on every wave, and find your eternity in each moment. Fools stand on their island of opportunities and look toward another land. There is no other land; there is no other life but this."

— *Henry David Thoreau*

CHAPTER SIX
BELIEVE THE INVISIBLE

> The antidote to frustration is a calm faith, not in your own cleverness, or in hard toil, but in God's guidance.
>
> — *Norman Vincent Peale*

Faith "believes." Some people exercise faith in family, their jobs, friends, or ther government. Some have faith in their creations—a car, house, or tool—and some have faith in other gods.

Being in prison, you may come to the conclusion that faith in God is usually practiced by pedophiles to get out of their work assignment; they go to the chapel to be protected, or to pass tobacco and drugs and manipulate the police so that their bid won't be hard. You would be partially right; some guys are pedophiles and users—they use the concept of faith for personal gain. We've all seen it: bibles on the bed so that the CO's won't trash their stuff.

I have searched a lot of cells and found bibles fixed to a certain section; you try and turn a page and read it, and the pages go right back to where it has been open to for years. So I understand the resistance to this conversation.

As you know, mankind is a three-part being: body, soul, and spirit. I think you would agree that all of us should seek to be healthy in all three of these areas. That is why I have decided to include a chapter on faith to address the soul from a Christian perspective. The main body of this chapter is written by a personal friend of mine, Brent Charles. Brent is an army veteran of Charlie Battery 2nd Battalion, 321st Field Artillery, of the 82nd Airborne.

He now lives in New Hampshire. Some who have read this script say that it sounds preachy. It probably does; he's a preacher. Brent's message explains faith, and his life story is a testament of the power of faith to change people, and I always find his story interesting. I hope that you will too.

WHAT IS FAITH?

Faith in the "English" language simply means "believes."

According to "Thayer's Greek/English Lexicon" the "Biblical" sense of faith focuses on the following: 1) conviction of the truth of anything, belief; in the NT of a conviction or belief respecting man's relationship to God and divine things, generally with the included idea of trust and holy fervor born of faith and joined with it. 2) Fidelity, faithfulness

So when we read from Hebrews 13:1 that

"Faith is the substance of things hoped for and the evidence of things not yet seen," we understand that the Biblical sense of faith is:

"A conviction that God (who we do not see) has promised a better life (we cannot see) through a means we do not fully understand and yet are called upon to trust and believe."

Many people, when confronted with the subject of faith, believe it is for persons who only desire to escape from reality or make excuse for their lives as they are. What many do not understand is that *"Faith, true Bible faith, comes from God and therefore is enduring and un-explainable."*

True saving faith from God (Ephesians 2:8, 9) causes all who experience it to exercise an irrational "Optimism" of their future that many see as escapism.

This leads us to the subject of "who has faith?"

WHO HAS FAITH?

All people exercise some kind of faith, even if only to trust that their car tires are not going to "blow" at high speeds on the interstate. But few people have "Bible" faith from God to believe that their wrecked, sinful, and wicked lives can be changed and that they have a better future to look forward to.

It is only this type of faith that brings an "Optimistic" view of your life, surroundings, and future. It is a faith that causes you to trust God in all of life's hardships and challenges.

One night a house caught fire and a young boy was forced to flee to the roof. The father stood on the ground below with outstretched arms, calling to his son, "Jump! I'll catch you." He knew the boy had to jump to save his life. All the boy could see, however, was flame, smoke, and blackness. As can be imagined, he was afraid to leave the roof. His father kept yelling: "Jump! I will catch you." But the boy protested, "Daddy, I can't see you." The father replied, "But I can see you and that's all that matters."

Ephesians 2:1-9 says:

> *"And you He made alive, who were dead in trespasses and sins (lying, stealing, murdering, adultery...), in which you once walked according to the course of this*

world, according to the prince of the power of the air (Satan), the spirit who now works in the sons of disobedience, among whom also we all once conducted ourselves in the lusts of our flesh, fulfilling the desires of the flesh and of the mind, and were by nature children of wrath, just as the others. "But God, who is rich in mercy, because of His great love with which He loved us, even when we were dead in trespasses, made us alive together with Christ (by grace you have been saved), and raised us up together, and made us sit together in the heavenly places in Christ Jesus, that in the ages to come He might show the exceeding riches of His grace in His kindness toward us in Christ Jesus. For by grace you have been saved through faith, and that not of yourselves; it is the gift of God, not of works, lest anyone should boast."

— Ephesians 2:1-9

God gives "saving faith." Those who possess that type of faith are His children. They recognize that their faith is "...not of themselves—but the gift of God!"

Have you considered why you are thinking of God at this time in your life? Why are you reading this book? Could it be that God has given to you the "faith" to believe and that He is drawing you to Himself with "Bands of love..." (Hosea 11:4).

That He desires you to be His child and has given you the "power to believe? Consider these words from the Apostle John:

"He (Jesus) was in the world, and the world was made through Him (that's right, Jesus made the World), and the world did not know Him. He came to His own (the Jews), and His own did not receive Him. But as many as received Him (you and me), to them He gave the right (literally the "power") to become children of God, to those who believe (have faith in) in His name (Jesus' name): who were born, not of blood, nor of the will of the flesh, nor of the will of man, (that is by a human mother and father) but of God (spiritually through faith given)." (John 1:10-13)

People who have "saving faith" are people who endure great hardship of body, soul, and spirit because they know! Somehow, some way they know!

That God is real, His Son Jesus Christ died for their sin, and therefore they have much to look forward to in life—despite the hardships!

David, a 2-year old with leukemia, was taken by his mother, Deborah, to Massachusetts General Hospital in Boston, to see Dr. John Truman who specializes in treating children with cancer and various blood diseases. Dr. Truman's prognosis was devastating: "He has a 50-50 chance."

The countless clinic visits, the blood tests, the intravenous drugs, the fear and pain—the mother's ordeal can be almost as bad as the child's because she must stand by, unable to bear the pain herself. David never cried in the waiting room, and although his friends in the clinic had to hurt him and stick needles in him, he hustled in ahead of his mother with a smile, sure of the welcome he always got. When he was three, David had to have a spinal tap—a painful procedure at any age. It was explained to him that, because he was sick, Dr. Truman had to do something to make him better. "If it hurts, remember it's because he loves you," Deborah said. The procedure was horrendous. It took three nurses to hold David still, while he yelled and sobbed and struggled. When it was almost over, the tiny boy, soaked in sweat and tears, looked up at the doctor and gasped, "Thank you, Dr. Toomas, for my hurting."

— *Monica Dickens, Miracles of Courage, 1985.*

WHY IS FAITH NEEDED?

You are reading this book because you are transitioning from a life behind bars where your freedoms were restricted and, for some, grossly taken away by force. You are reading this book because you made poor decisions that lead to your incarceration. You may be reading this book having been falsely accused. You may be reading this book because you did something justifiable—but deemed reckless.

I tell you, by faith, that you are reading this book because God desires you to be His child! Set free from sin and its effect upon your life!

You need faith! Faith in God and His eternal love! Faith that will give you a new outlook on life and lead you in paths of good for God's sake!

Your family needs faith. Your friends need faith. Your very future depends upon the faith you exercise right now, in God and no other. Saving faith that will help you to understand:

When family turns you away—God will take me in (Psalm 27:10).

When jobs are hard to find—God will provide (Psalm 37:25).

When peace seems impossible—God will give it to you (Isaiah 26:3).

When funds are short and you want a fast buck—(Proverbs 18:9).

When anger makes you want to "payback" wrongs you have endured—(Romans 12:19).

Most of all, you will need faith to believe on the Lord Jesus Christ for salvation, and that, my friend, will completely change your life! How do I know? Here is my story of faith.

My home life was rough. Dad, a Vietnam era vet, was a drinker. This made for a lot of tension in the home. Dad was fighter too. This made for a lot of stress and confrontation. When I became a teenager I followed his path: drugs, alcohol, fighting, and fast money.

After riding shotgun to pick up a package outside Boston, my friend and I were paid in dope and cash. As we left the apartment building we did not know that federal and local agents were about to arrest everyone left in the building. They all went to prison for whatever was in the package plus grand theft auto, money laundering, and the like.

Despite the close brush with the law I did not slow down. Things got worse.

I became bolder with weed, hash, speed, coke, acid, and lots of beer to wash it down. I was selfish and focused on one thing—women! Another year went by. I had been kicked out of the house (for something I did not do!) and was on my own. Family took me in and I worked hard at school and my concrete job. But I partied hard too!

After a stint in Wyoming I returned home and the thought struck me that my life was a mess. I decided to join the Army and get away from all the chaos.

The military was good for me. I detoxed in basic (major suck pill too), and then in jump school at Ft. Benning I had a major acid trip just before a night jump that freaked me out. But all in all I was clean and sober— three months! After arriving at my duty station I drank again, smoked pot (off duty), and occasionally hit the coke (recreationally of course).

Two years into my time with Uncle Sam a sergeant was moving out of our barracks and needed help moving all his stuff from the 3rd floor to a truck. Me and a couple guys helped thinking we would get a rack of beer for payment— instead we were given Bibles.

I could not stop reading that thing! Day and night, all I could do was read, read, and read.

I got married; we had a son, and I drank a little but laid off most of the shit.

Then I had a really bad accident that nearly wiped me out for good. While in the hospital a chaplain visited and gave me a Bible, and after he left I began to read. All of a sudden I had the thought come over me:

If you have a bad jump and your chute does not open your body may bounce on impact but your soul is going straight to hell!

I was scared shitless! What was happening? Why did I think that? I began talking to God, bargaining with Him, and then I remembered having read in the Bible:

> *But at midnight Paul and Silas were praying and singing hymns to God, and the prisoners were listening to them. Suddenly there was a great earthquake, so that the foundations of the prison were shaken; and immediately all the doors were opened and everyone's chains were loosed. And the keeper of the prison, awaking from sleep and seeing the prison doors open, supposing the prisoners had fled, drew his sword and was about to kill himself. But Paul called with a loud voice, saying, "Do yourself no harm, for we are all here." Then he called for a light, ran in, and fell down trembling before Paul and Silas. And he brought them out and said, "Sirs, what must I do to be saved?" So they said, "Believe on the Lord Jesus Christ, and you will be saved, you and your household."*

> *— Acts 16:25-31*

In that moment I knew the Bible was true, I was in trouble, and on the fast track to hell! I cried out to God for mercy and told Him what a jerk I was. I asked Him to save me and take control of my life. That was in 1987. I have now been married 31 years to the same woman, and I have 4 grown children and 4 grandsons with another on the way.

I have owned two great businesses, went to college at age 30, pastored a wonderful church, and I now am a missionary.

We have had some bumps, real crap too, but through it all I am able to be optimistic because I have "Faith" in God. Do you have faith? Do you believe the things you have read so far? If so, I encourage you to exercise that faith now and cry out to God for Him to save you. It will forever change your life.

CHAPTER SEVEN
WHAT'S YOUR PLAN

"The Victory of Success is half won when one gains the habit of setting and achieving goals."

— *Og Mandino*

One day I struck up a conversation with this inmate named Mann who was working for me. We were talking about goals, as he had heard me talking with another inmate about my 30/60/90 Plan. We talked for a few minutes, and I soon came to understand that I was out of touch with reality. For some of you, a mere seven days is a long time, let alone 30, 60, and 90 days.

You might be asking, *"What is a 30/60/90 plan?"*

I developed this plan after years of watching inmates ride through their sentence without making any plans for their release. The 30/60/90 represents short term goals. I would find out that a particular inmate was getting out and go speak with him:

"Hey man, what's your plan?"

"I got plans, Officer Johnmeyer."

"Oh yeah, let me see them."

They responded by pointing to their head. That is basically worthless! Right now you're not overly worried about paying rent, buying groceries, or making sure that you have car insurance, but when you get out, all of that will come crashing down on you. I have seen a lot of guys run their time right down to the wire, then talk smack in the dorm or on the vents for the last six months. Wouldn't it be wise to begin to think about your EOS carefully, seek council, create and write down workable goals, review them, and rewrite them until you are at peace? Your future is at stake.

Check out this article from *Success* Magazine with an interview between Jim Cathcart, Cynthia Kersey, and Brian Tracy (with thanks to Cynthia Kersey for her permission to reprint+):

HOW TO SET A GOAL AND ACHIEVE IT

Jim Cathcart, Cynthia Kersey, and Brian Tracy weigh in on how to achieve your goals.

Jim Cathcart is a professional speaker and founder of the Cathcart Institute Inc. His top-selling books include *Relationship Selling* and *The Acorn Principle*.

Brian Tracy is a top management consultant and author of more than 45 books, including the best-selling *Goals: How to Get Everything You Want—Faster Than You Ever Thought Possible*.

Cynthia Kersey is the best-selling author of *Unstoppable: 45 Powerful Stories of Perseverance and Triumph from*

People Just like You, as well as a performance and productivity coach.

Q: Why set goals?

Brian Tracy: All successful people are intensely goal-oriented. They know what they want and they are focused single-mindedly on achieving it, every single day. Your ability to set goals is the master skill of success. Goals unlock your positive mind and release ideas and energy for goal attainment. Without goals, you simply drift and flow on the currents of life. With goals, you fly like an arrow, straight and true to your target.

One of the rules for success is this: It doesn't matter where you're coming from; all that matters is where you're going. And where you are going is solely determined by you and your thoughts. Clear goals increase confidence, develop your competence and boost your levels of motivation.

Cynthia Kersey: One of my favorite quotes is by Abraham Lincoln: "The best way to predict your future is to create it." Setting goals provides us with a way to create our future today by focusing our attention and daily action steps toward what we really want and then making them a reality. Making a decision to set goals, put them in motion is something that works.

Q: Why do I keep setting goals and failing to see them through to fruition?

Brian Tracy: Most people give up before they even make the first try. And the reason they give up is because of all the obstacles, difficulties, problems and roadblocks that immediately appear as soon as they decide to do something they have never done before. The fact is that successful people fail far more often than unsuccessful people. Successful people try more things, fall down, pick themselves up and try again—over and over before they finally win.

The two major obstacles to achievement are fear and self-doubt. The fear of failure, poverty, loss, embarrassment or rejection holds most people back from trying in the first place. Small fears overwhelm them and, like a bucket of water on a small fire, extinguish their desire completely.

The second mental obstacle, closely aligned to fear, is self-doubt. We doubt our own abilities. We compare ourselves unfavorably to others and think that others are somehow better, smarter and more competent than we are. We think "I'm not good enough." We feel inadequate and inferior to the challenges of achieving the great goals that we so want to accomplish. If there is anything good about doubt and fear, it is that they are learned emotions. And whatever has been learned can be unlearned through practice and repetition.

Q: Is there anything I should think about before sitting down to write my goals?

Cynthia Kersey: Before sitting down to actually write your list of goals, I encourage you to first take a moment to discover something deeper—your purpose. What gives your life meaning and gives you personal satisfaction? What are the unique gifts and insights that you can contribute to your world? Your purpose will fuel your efforts and give you the drive to continue in the pursuit of your goals, no matter the challenges.

Start by writing How I Want to Be Remembered. List the qualities, deeds and characteristics for which you would like to be remembered by your friends, spouse, children, co-workers, the community, and even the world. If you have special relationships with other people or groups, such as a church or synagogue, club or team, include them on the list, too. You will begin to uncover your true values and the sources of meaning in your life. Being clear about your purpose may be your single most important accomplishment.

Q: OK, I have a goal list, now what?

Jim Cathcart: Figure out which items matter more than all of the rest. Ask yourself, "If I got this one, wouldn't all of the others come along for the ride?" Often, when we achieve our one big goal, we get a whole truckload of other goals as part of the process. Don't worry about achieving all of them, just make sure you achieve the few that you really care about. The others will come.

Brian Tracy: Plan.

Make a list of everything that you can think of that you will have to do to achieve your goal. Organize your list by priority. Organize your list by sequence. What must be done before something else is done? Determine how much time and money it will take to achieve your goal or complete your task. Revisit and revise your plan accordingly.

Q: What advice do you have for helping me stick with my goals throughout an entire year?

Jim Cathcart: Manage your mindset. Surround yourself with people and things that keep you focused. Take charge of whom you spend the most time with. Manage your workspace and home settings so that you are reminded of your goals and your commitments. Form habits that lead you to becoming the person you'll need to be. When you form the habit of starting your productivity earlier in the day, associating with more positive people, managing the news and information you feed your mind, controlling the language you use especially the ways in which you describe yourself—you will find it easier to succeed. Become the person who would achieve your goals and who would deserve them.

It is extremely important to put what you have just read into action. For some, including myself, it may seem pointless to sit down and write out a plan to achieve your hopes and dreams. Sometimes I think I can just go and do it! That's fine in a perfect world with no distractions, but in my life and yours there are distractions.

What do distractions do? They distract, pulling us off point, off the road to our dreams.

"When obstacles arise you change your direction to reach your goals; you do not change your decision to get there."

— *Zig Zigler*

So if a 30/60/90 goal plan works for you then great! Go with that! If that plan is too far out for you, then make your short term goals smaller and more focused. You may need to scale it down to a 7/15/30 goal plan. Once you have followed through to completion the plan that you have written out with your hands, it will motivate you, pulling you away from the jailhouse to your dreams.

CHAPTER EIGHT
YOUR STORY

"If you would not be forgotten as soon as you are dead, either write something worth reading or do something worth writing."

— *Benjamin Franklin*

As I sit here and ponder the last chapter of my book, I wonder *"What can I say that will stay with them as they close the last page? What will they tell their friends?"* The word that comes to mind is "Legacy." I have talked with the guys that work for me in the kitchen many times about this subject. Legacy is the story *you*, the reader, leave behind. Legacy is about life and living. It's about learning from the past, living in the present, and building for the future.

Where do you think it's best to plant a young tree: a clearing in an old-growth forest or an open field? Ecologists tell us that a young tree grows better when it's planted in an area with older trees. The reason, it seems, is that the roots of the young tree are able to follow the pathways created by former trees and implant themselves more deeply. Over time, the roots of many trees may actually graft themselves to one another, creating an intricate, interdependent foundation hidden under the ground. In this way, stronger trees share resources with weaker ones so that the whole forest becomes healthier. That's legacy: an interconnection across time, with a need for those who have come before us and a responsibility to those who come after us.

Legacy is fundamental to what it is to be human. Research shows that without a sense of working to create a legacy, adults lose meaning in their life.

My great-grandfather Albert's dad came from Germany as an immigrant and settled in the farmlands of Missouri. The name Johnmeyer quickly became synonymous with honesty and hard work. That last name meant something, and my family set out to extend that into the next generation, and now I'm seeking to pass those values on to my son.

What about you? When you sign your name on anything—a contract or a check—does it mean something, or is it just ink on a piece of paper?

Some of the new guys coming into my kitchen are sometimes given a voluntary assignment, and this can be your assignment. If you could pick any five words in the dictionary to describe your last name, What would they be? You only get five, so make them count. I have listed some strong words for you to consider.

- Honorable
- Loving
- Merciful

- Approachable
- Intelligent
- Selfless
- Passionate
- Loyal
- Honest
- Hard Working
- Thoughtful
- Forgiving

Some of you may not have come from good families. That's okay; it simply means you have an opportunity to write your story the way you want your last name to be remembered. Give those five words some serious thought, and then go out and begin to act out those five words in your day to day life. We have to purpose "Legacy"; it doesn't just happen.

We have to share life lessons and moments of revelation with our children, teach them and encourage them to represent their name, the one you gave to them.

When your time has come and gone, let it be said to your children and your children's children, *"I remember your dad, or mom. They were good people."*

Remember the comment made in the Foreword, *"Your story is only as good as the last person who tells it."* The day you step out is the beginning of a new chapter. *"Go write, a memorable one!"* Be blessed.

BIBLIOGRAPHY

Albrecht, K. P. (2012, March 22). BrainSnacks. Retrieved September 16, 2015, from Psychology Today: https://www.psychologytoday.com/blog/brainsnacks/201 203/the-only-5-fears-we-all-share

Association, A. P. (n.d.). meditate. (n.d.). Dictionary.com Unabridged. Retrieved September 16, 2015, from Dictionary.com: http://dictionary.reference.com/browse/meditate

Cathcart, J., Tracy, B., & Kersey, C. (n.d.). article/1-on-1-how-to-set-a-goal-and-achieve-it. Retrieved September 16, 2015, from http://www.success.com: http://www.success.com/article/1-on-1-how-to-set-a-goal-and-achieve-it

Dr. Steve McSwain. (n.d.). How to Control Your Mind and Thoughts. Retrieved September 16, 2015, from Beliefnet: http://www.beliefnet.com/Inspiration/Articles/How-to-Control-Your-Mind-and-Thoughts.aspx

Horn, S. (2013, August 16th). Singing Changes your Brain. Retrieved October 30, 2015, from Time Magazine: http://ideas.time.com/2013/08/16/singing-changes-your-brain/

Jameson, R. C. (2014, April 28). Be Careful of Your Thoughts: They Control Your Destiny. Retrieved September 16, 2015, from Huffington Post: http://www.huffingtonpost.com/robert-c-jameson/be-careful-of-your-though_b_5214689.html

Jobs That Hire Felons. (n.d.). List of Jobs for Felons. Retrieved September 17, 2015, from: http://jobsthathirefelons.org/

PH.d, B. M. (2013, May 07). Stop Fighting your Negative Thoughts. Retrieved October 30, 2015, from Psychology Today: https://www.psychologytoday.com/blog/shyness-is-nice/201305/stop-fighting-your-negative-thoughts

Susan V. Bosak. (n.d.). What is Legacy? Retrieved September 25, 2015, from Legacy Project: http://www.legacyproject.org/guides/whatislegacy.html

Tierney, J. (2011, November 21). "A Serving of Gratitude May Save the Day". Retrieved September 16, 2015, from New York Times: http://www.nytimes.com/2011/11/22/science/a-serving-of-gratitude-brings-healthy-dividends.html?_r=0#

ABOUT THE AUTHOR

Chance Johnmeyer is a prison officer with a colorful past—in that he's worked an interesting combination of jobs. A United States Air Force veteran, he has also been employed as a carpenter, factory worker, and commercial flower grower. He's also studied theology and traveled the world, including Japan, Korea, and England. He has taken his 48 years of varied life experience, which includes 22 years of marriage, and combined it in his first book, *Unlocked: Keys to Getting Out & Staying Out.* He currently lives in Milton, Florida, with his family.

RESOURCE GUIDE

STATE OF FLORIDA

SUGGESTED READING LIST

FOR THE SPACE BETWEEN THE NOTES

1.) *Conversations with God: An Uncommon Dialogue, Book 1*
Written by Neale Donald Walsch, copyright 1996

2.) *Richest Man in Babylon*
Written by George S. Clason, copyright January 2002

3.) *Think and Grow Rich*
Written by Napolean Hill, revised and updated August 2005

4.) *Way of the Peaceful Warrior a Book That Changes Lives*
Written by Dan Millman, HS Kramer, 2006

5.) *As a Man Thinketh*
Written by James Allen, November 2014

6.) *The Seasons of Life*
Written by Jim Rohn, June 1981

7.) *The One Minute Manager*
Written by Kenneth Blanchard PhD, May 2015

HARDSHIP LICENSE

If you have a suspended license in the state of Florida, follow the steps below to obtain a hardship license so you can drive legally while getting your license back.

Sign up for an online 12-hour Advanced Driving School (ADI) class. One you've paid, you will receive a letter of enrollment.

Go to the clerk of court and get a "30 day search" of your driving record. This takes just a few minutes and they will give you a letter that provides information about your driving record.

After you've received the letter of enrollment from the traffic school and a letter from the clerk, you can go to the DMV and apply for a hardship license with a hearing officer.

You'll still need to complete the 12-hour course within the deadline set by the DMV. If you are a "habitual offender" as indicated in the DMV letter of enrollment, you must complete the course before you can apply for the hardship license.

Start Now!

ONLINE TRAFFIC SCHOOL BENEFITS

Take the course online course from the convenience and privacy of your home or work—no classroom necessary.

Simple to use, no computer experience needed.

Unlimited log-ins and log-outs so you can complete the course at your convenience, in your spare time.

Get the certificate you need to get your full license back via email.

Start Now!

THE RULES

The steps above are for drivers that have had their license suspended in the state of Florida for points, as a habitual traffic offender (non-DUI related), or by court order. Some violations are not eligible for a hardship license:

- Suspended license for being incapable of operating a motor vehicle safely. Suspension is for one year. You are not eligible for a hardship license.

- Conviction for Driving Under the Influence (DUI).Suspension is for 180 days - 1 year. DUI School completion and treatment, if referred, is required. You then can apply for a hardship license in any Administrative Reviews Office where you live.

HOUSING RESOURCES FOR THE HOMELESS

Seek to make contact with these resources. If they are unable to house you for any reason, just ask a representative from the organization you are in touch with, if they may have some suggestions of other resources. It's very important to not compare the conditions set forth by these groups with your previous incarceration. They have been established to help you.

LOCAL COALITIONS

(Not Housing for Urban Development designated lead agencies, but working with homeless people in their counties)

Citrus
John Young Hunger and Homeless Coalition of Citrus County
PO Box 447, Homosassa Springs, FL 34447
hhcocc@gmail.com

Glades, Hendry
Erica Villafuerte Hendry/Glades Homeless Coalition
117 Fort Thompson Ave., LaBelle, FL 37935
ericav@gladescofl.net
hendrygladeshomelesscoalition@yahoo.com

Lee
Janet Bartos Lee County Homeless Coalition
1500 Colonial Blvd., Suite 221, Fort Myers, FL 33907
leehomeless@gmail.com leehomeless.org

Manatee
Adell Erozer Turning Points
701 17th Ave. W, Bradenton, FL 34205
aerozer@tpmanatee.org
www.tpmanatee.org

Miami-Dade
Miami Coalition for the Homeless, Bobbie Ibarra, Director
3550
Biscayne Blvd., Suite 610, Miami, FL 33137

Nassau
Coalition for the Homeless of Nassau County
P.O. Box 16123, Fernandina Beach, FL, 32034

Okaloosa
Okaloosa Coalition for the Homeless, Martha Lackey,
President
8-B Bobolink St., P.O. Box 5589, Ft. Walton Beach, FL
32549

Palm Beach
Marilyn L. Munoz, Executive Director Homeless Coalition
Liaison for Homeless Advisory Board
810 Datura St. W, Palm Beach, FL 34401
P: 561-355-4764
F: 561-242-7339
http://www.homelesscoalitionpbc.org
homelesscoalitionpbc@gmail.com
http://www.facebook.com/homelesscoalitionpbc
http://www.twitter.com/homelesscoalitionpbc

FEDERAL BONDING

The Federal Bonding Program is an incentive program that allows employers to hire with limited liability to their business at-risk job applicants. A Federal Fidelity Bond, supplied by Travelers Insurance Co., is a business insurance policy that insures the employer for theft, forgery, larceny, or embezzlement by the bonded employee.

The bond does not cover liability due to poor workmanship, job injuries, or work accidents. The Federal Bonding Program does not provide bail bonds or court bonds for the legal system, nor do they providecontract bonds, performance bonds, or license bonds that are sometimes needed for self-employment.

ELIGIBILITY REQUIREMENTS

At-risk job applicants are:

- Ex-offenders
- Recovering substance abusers (alcohol or drugs)
- Welfare recipients and other persons having poor financial credit, or who have declared bankruptcy

- Economically disadvantaged youth and adults who lack a work history
- Individuals dishonorably discharged from the military
- Anyone who cannot secure employment without bonding services

Employed workers who need bonding services to avoid layoff or to secure a promotion are also eligible.

All employers are eligible for bonding services. Bonds can be issued as soon as the applicant has a job offer and a scheduled start date.

Bonds are in units of $5,000 and provide coverage for a six-month period. When the initial bond coverage expires, employers can purchase continued bond coverage from Travelers Insurance Co. if workers demonstrated job honesty under bond coverage provided by the Federal Bonding Program. One unit of bond insurance coverage is usually sufficient to cover most job applicants.

HOW TO APPLY

Contact your local Career Source Florida center for more information and an application form or visit the Federal Bonding Program website. http://www.bonds4jobs.com/

GETTING A JOB

Getting out into the job market fresh out of prison is not going to be a fun time. If you're not returning to a previous employer that has agreed to hire you back, your job search will seem almost impossible. Understand up front that those just getting out of prison are more likely to be rejected numerous times. You must commit now to *not giving up*; knowing you will face flat out rejection, empty promises, and rude people. Stick to your course.

The single most important thing you need from your first job is not salary or a high wage per hour. The most important thing you need to advance your future is job history. Many of you have no job history. Most prospective employers will assume that you are not trustworthy because you have no job history. You may have to take on a job that you don't like, one that requires long hours, sweat, and dirt, but it is not without gain. Your choice to stick it out for 6 months or a year will be wise, a vital part of the road to proving to yourself and to future employers that you are serious about your future.

There will be competing voices along the way. They will be in your head, saying things like, "You're a failure; remember last time?" And there will be voices on the outside, quite possibly you friends and family, saying things like, "Hey bro, deliver this for me, and I'll take care of you." These voices are your enemy, not your friend, and you must deal with them accordingly.

If you don't owe the state or feds any more time, you are as "free" as you will ever be. Cherish that, cherish your children, their laughter, the color green, a sky full of stars each night—you have a responsibility to yourself and others. Take it! You've done your time.

Think of all the companies and businesses in your area. Make a list of your 10 most desired jobs now, and then back that up with a secondary 10. Put that aside for your job search, and then when you get out start checking them off by putting in applications. Do your homework before you go. Complete a master application with previous places of employment, past names of supervisors, addresses, and contact numbers. Make a list of your character references (people that can vouch for you being a hard worker) and their contact numbers.

Below I have included a list of possible employers from the web-site jobsthathirefelons.org.

You will have to check out each company's hiring website, do the research, and follow the application process like normal.

- Aamco
- Ace Hardware
- Allied Van Lines
- American Greetings
- Anderson Windows
- Apple Inc.
- Aramark
- AT&T
- Avis Rent a Car
- Avon Products
- Baskin-Robbins
- Bed, Bath & Beyond
- Black & Decker
- Blue Cross & Blue Shield Association
- Braum's Inc.
- Bridgestone

- Budget Rent a Car
- Buffalo Wild Wings
- Campbell's Soup
- Canon
- Carl's Jr
- Caterpillar Inc.
- CDW
- Chilis
- Chipotle
- Cintas
- Community Education Centers
- ConAgra Foods
- Dairy Queen
- Delta Faucet
- Denny's
- Dole Food Company
- Dollar Rent a Car
- Dollar Tree
- Dr. Pepper
- Dunlop Tires
- Dunkin' Donuts
- DuPont
- Duracell
- Epson
- ERMCO, Inc.
- Family Dollar
- Firestone
- Complete Auto Care

- Pilot Flying J
- Fruit of the Loom
- Fujifilm
- General Electric
- General Mills
- Georgia-Pacific
- Goodwill
- Grainger
- Greyhound
- Hanes
- Hilton Hotels
- Home Depot
- IBM
- In-N-Out Burger
- Jack in the Box
- K-Mart
- Kelly Moore Paints
- KFC
- Kohl's
- Kraft Foods
- Kroger
- Longhorn Steakhouse
- Lowe's
- LSG Sky Chefs
- McDonald's
- Men's Wearhouse
- Metals USA
- Miller

- Brewing Company
- Motorola
- The New York Times
- Olive Garden
- PepsiCo
- Phillip Morris Inc.
- Pilgrim's
- Red Lobster
- Red Robin
- Safeway
- Trader Joes
- Tyson Foods
- U-Haul
- US Steal Corporation
- Volunteers of America
- Walgreens
- Wendy's
- Wyndham Hotels
- Salvation Army
- Sara Lee
- Sears
- Shell Oil
- Shoprite
- Sony
- Subway
- Toys "R" Us
- Xerox
- Albertsons

- Applebee's
- Bahama Breeze
- Best Western
- Carrier Corporation
- Chick-fil-A
- Chrysler
- Dart Containers
- Deer Park Spring Water
- Eddie Vs
- Prime Seafood
- Embassy Suites
- Food Services of America
- Frito-Lay
- Genentech
- Golden Corral
- Great Clips
- HH Gregg
- IHOP
- Ikea
- J.B. Hunt Transport
- Jiffy Lube
- Jimmy Johns
- Nordstrom
- O'Charleys
- Pactiv
- Pappadeaux
- PetSmart
- Preferred Freezer Services

- Praxair
- Radisson
- Restaurant Depot
- Reyes Beverage Group
- Rubbermaid
- Seasons 52
- Sysco
- Teleperformance
- Tesla
- US Foods
- WinCo Foods

RESEARCH LINKS FOR POSSIBLE EMPLOYMENT OPPORTUNITIES.

These are links detail major upcoming construction projects for those with experience in this field. Simply contact the appropriate entity and ask for the name of the contractor who was granted the bid to complete the work. This will then allow you to access the contractors website to search for job openings and requirements for your area.

http://www.dot.state.fl.us/publicinformationoffice/moreDOT/majorprojects.shtm

http://www.cmdgroup.com/market-intelligence/articles/twenty-major-upcoming-california-and-florida-construction-projects-u.s.-feb

http://www.bizjournals.com/orlando/blog/2015/07/utility-crews-prep-for-sunrail-phase-2.html

http://www.orlandosentinel.com/business/os-orlando-international-airport-expansion-begins-2015

The following is for informational purposes only, provided to the author by Federal Student Aid.

Thank you for your inquiry about federal student aid.

The U.S. Department of Education's (ED's) major financial aid programs help students pay for education beyond high school.

Our StudentAid.gov website provides details about ED's financial aid programs, eligibility criteria, application procedures, and award levels.

The following information explains how a criminal conviction might affect a student's eligibility for federal student aid:

* Federal student aid eligibility is suspended for students convicted under federal or state law of sale or possession of drugs that occurred while they were receiving federal student aid. The length of the suspension is based on the type and number of offenses. A student can regain eligibility by satisfactorily completing an approved drug rehabilitation program.

* Federal aid eligibility may also be suspended for students who received a judgment under the Anti-Drug Abuse Act of 1988, which

includes provisions that authorize federal and state judges to deny certain federal benefits-- including student aid--to persons convicted of drug trafficking or possession.

* A student is ineligible for a Federal Pell Grant if he or she is subject to an involuntary civil commitment after completing a period of incarceration for a forcible or non-forcible sexual offense.

Other types of criminal convictions are not considered in determining a student's eligibility for federal student aid.

However, federal student aid is limited for incarcerated students. For more information, review our fact sheet at http://studentaid.ed.gov/sites/default/files/ai d-info-for-incarcerated-individuals.pdf.

For more information, a student should contact the financial aid office at the school in which he or she plans to enroll.

We hope this information is helpful.

E-Mail Unit
StudentAid.gov
Federal Student Aid

WELDING SCHOOLS

1.) **Tulsa Welding School**
3500 Southside Blvd., Jacksonville, FL 32216
Accredited with pipe welding, blueprint reading, and welder certifications.

2.) **Southeastern Welding School**
6973 Highway Ave., Unit 107,Jacksonville, FL 32254

3.) **Atlantic Technical Center Welder Training Program**
4700 Coconut Creek Parkway, Coconut Creek, FL 33063
Accredited with advanced pipe welding, advanced blueprint reading, and AWS welder certifications.

4.) **College of Central Florida Welding Program**
3001 SW College Rd., Ocala, FL 34474
Accredited with pipe welding, blueprint reading, and welder certifications.

5.) **Southern Technical College – Welding Program**
a.)Orlando Campus: 1485 Florida Mall Ave., Orlando, FL 32809
b.)Sanford Campus: 2910 S Orlando Dr., Sanford, FL 32773
Accredited with pipe welding, blueprint reading, and welder certifications. This school offers an Associate of Science Degree in Welding Technology!

6.) **CDA Technical Institute – Maritime Welding Program**

1 Trout River Dr., Jacksonville, FL 32208
Accredited with pipe welding, blueprint reading, and welder certifications.

7.) **Mid Florida Tech Welder Training**
2900 W Oak Ridge Rd., Orlando, Florida 32809
Accredited with pipe welding, blueprint reading, and welder certifications (AWS, ASME and API).

8.) **Washington-Holmes Technical Center – Welding School**
757 Hoyt St. Chipley, Florida 32428
Accredited with pipe welding and blueprint reading.

HVAC SCHOOLS

(Heating, Ventilation, Air Conditioning)
1.) **Florida HVAC Technical School**
41 N Orlando Ave., #100, Cocoa Beach, Fl. 32931

2.) **Erwin Technical Center**
2010 E Hillsborough Ave., Tampa, Fl. 33610

3.) **Southern Technical College**
298 Havendale Blvd., Auburndale, FL 33823

4.) **Palm Construction School**
7448 Universal Blvd, Orlando, FL 32819

5.) **US Solar Institute**
8242 W State Rd. 84, Davie, FL 33324

6.) **US Solar Institute**
1024 NE 43rd Ct., Oakland Park, FL 33334

7.) **US Solar Institute**
ussolarinstitute.com
913 Ne 4th Ave, Fort Lauderdale, FL 33304

CULINARY SCHOOLS

1.) **Aprons Cooking School**
5050 Champion Blvd., Boca Raton, FL 33496

2.) **Florida Culinary Institute**
2410 Metrocentre Blvd., West Palm Beach, FL 33407

3.) **Le Cordon Bleu College of Culinary Arts**
3221 Enterprise Way, Miramar, FL 33025

4.) **Publix Aprons Cooking School**
7835 Gunn Hwy., Tampa, FL 33626

CORRECTIONAL EDUCATION

Since 1974, Ohio University's Correctional Education has provided an opportunity for incarcerated students to study through print-based courses, to earn college credit, and work toward an Ohio University degree.

Students who want to learn — but aren't interested in a degree — can take a few courses or complete a legal studies certificate. View the degree and certificate options below:

Associate degrees
Bachelor's degree
Legal Studies Certificate Courses

Ohio University Correctional Education, Haning Hall 102, 1 Ohio University, Athens OH 45701.

Please allow 2 to 3 weeks for inquiry packets to arrive.

Hi Chance

Thank you for contacting Opportunity@Work.

Re-wiring the demand side of U.S. labor market is the goal of Opportunity@Work, a civic enterprise based at New America. Employers are now experiencing a classic market failure, in which hiring and training practices are inadvertently limiting the collective talent pipeline and creating "skills mismatches" with economy-wide ripple effects. These mismatches are a key reason why nearly half of U.S. employers report difficulties hiring employees who have the skills their companies need to compete.

With such a broad goal in our sights, we are starting with information technology jobs, which constitute 12 percent of today's open jobs☐ —☐ over 680,000 of them–in the U.S. As part of the TechHire initiative President Obama launched in March 2015, Opportunity@Work has created a learning network for 35 communities from Wilmington to Chattanooga to Albuquerque. This network will help align employers to hire for middle-class IT jobs based on competence and readiness, rather than pedigree.

As a part of President Obama's TechHire initiative, over 30 communities are taking action – working with each other and national employers – to expand access to tech jobs for more Americans, including those with criminal records, with fast track training like coding boot camps and new recruitment and placement strategies.

Memphis, TN and New Orleans, LA are expanding TechHire programs to support people with criminal records.

Newark, NJ, working with the New Jersey Institute of Technology and employers like Audible, Panasonic, and Prudential, will offer training through the Art of Code program in software development with a focus on training and placement for formerly incarcerated people.

New Haven, CT, Justice Education Center, New Haven Works, and others will launch a pilot program to train and place individuals with criminal records, and will start a program to train incarcerated people in tech programming skills.

Washington, DC partners will train and place 200 formerly incarcerated people in tech jobs. They will engage IT companies to develop and/or review modifications to hiring processes that can be made for individuals with a criminal record.

Thanks again for contacting us!

Sincerely,
Deon

ENTREPRENEUR/SELF EMPLOYMENT

Maybe you have the heart of an entrepreneur, and you're thinking about starting your own business. The State of Florida has many Small Business Development Centers throughout the state that are an invaluable resource, for planning a new business. They are staffed with experienced business analyst that will help walk you through the process of creating business plans, financials, and many other aspects of starting a new business. It's hard work, and can be very frustrating, but with proper planning your dream can become reality. Contact one near your hometown. A successful business begins with a good plan.

FLORIDA SMALL BUSINESS DEVELOPMENT CENTERS

Orlando
3201 E Colonial Drive, Suite A-20
Orlando, FL 32803-5140

Kissimmee
1425 E Vine St
Kissimmee/Osceola County COC
Kissimmee, FL 34744-3621

Sanford
1445 Dolgner Place
Sanford, FL 32771-9204

Mount Dora
17521 US Highway 441, Suite #6
Mount Dora, FL 32757

Groveland
20763 US Highway 27
Groveland, FL 34736

Leesburg
600 Market St
Leesburg Business & Technology Center
Leesburg, FL 34748-5143

Lake Wales
201 W. Central Ave
Lake Wales City Hall
Lake Wales, FL 33853

Lakeland
35 Lake Morton Dr
Lakeland Chamber of Commerce, Park Trammell Building
Lakeland, FL 33802

Melbourne
3865 N Wickham Rd
Rm 117, Bldg. 10
Melbourne, FL 32935-2310

Daytona Beach
1200 W International Speedway Blvd
Daytona Beach, FL 32114-2817

Saint Leo
33701 State Road 52
Donald R. Tapia School of Business
Saint Leo, FL 33574

Ocala
3003 SW College Rd, Ste 105
Ocala, FL 34474-6253

Brooksville
15588 Aviation Loop Dr
Greater Hernando Chamber of Commerce
Brooksville, FL 34604-6801

Avon Park
600 W College Dr, Bldg T
South Florida Community College Avon Park, FL 33825-9356

Palm Coast
160 Cyprus Point Parkway, Suite B105
Palm Coast,
FL 32164-8436

Tampa – USF Connect
3802 Spectrum Blvd, Ste 111 USF Connect Building
Tampa, FL 33612

Tampa – Hillsborough County
75.4 miles
Entrepreneur Collaborative Center
2101 E. Palm Avenue
Tampa, FL 33605-3915

Crystal River
76.3 miles
Citrus County Office
915 N. Suncoast Boulevard
Crystal River, Florida 34429

Tampa
1101 Channelside Dr, Ste 210 Tampa, FL 33602-3613

Palatka
78.3 miles
1100 Reid Street
C/O Putnam County Chamber of Commerce
Palatka, FL 32177-3653

Vero Beach
6155 College Lane
IRSC Mueller Campus
Vero Beach, FL 32966

Clearwater
13805 58th St N, Ste 1-200
Clearwater, FL 33760-3716

St. Petersburg
140 7th Ave., South, Davis 108
St. Petersburg, Florida 33701

Gainesville
2153 SE Hawthorne Rd, Ste 139 Gainesville, FL 32641-7577

St. Augustine
96.9 miles
4040 Lewis Speedway
St. Augustine, FL 32084-8637

Fort Pierce
3209 Virginia Ave, Room Y101
Fort Pierce, FL 34981-5541

Bradenton
1112 Manatee Ave. East, Suites 245 & 246
Suncoast Workforce Building
Bradenton, FL 34208

North Port
5920 Pan American Blvd.
North Port, FL 34287

Port Charlotte
115.9 miles
2702 Tamiami Trail
Port Charlotte, FL 33952-5129

Jacksonville
University Center, 12000 Alumni Dr
Jacksonville, FL 32224-2677

Stuart
2400 SE Salerno Rd
Stuart, FL 34997-6505

Cape Coral
1020 Cultural Park Blvd, Unit 3
Cape Coral,, FL 33990

Palm Beach Gardens
3160 PGA Blvd
Palm Beach Gardens, FL 33410-2802

Yulee
96135 Nassau Place
Yulee, FL 32097-8635

Fort Myers
10501 FGCU Blvd South
CLI, Lutgert COB Unit 2320 Fort Myers, FL 33965-6502

Live Oak
212 North Ohio Avenue
Live Oak, FL 32064

Boca Raton
3000 Saint Lucie Ave, Ste AD303
Boca Raton, FL 33431-6418

Fort Lauderdale
111 E. Las Olas Blvd
Higher Education Complex, Rm 1010
Ft. Lauderdale, FL 33301

Miami
FIU Downtown on Brickell
1101 Brickell Avenue, South Tower Penthouse, 11th Floor
Miami, FL 33131

Tallahassee
2035 E Paul Dirac Dr
Morgan Bldg, Innovation Park Ste 130
Tallahassee, FL 32310-3700

Gretna
14615 E Main St
Gretna, FL 32332-4021

Key West
5901 College Rd, Room C-218 Key West, FL 33040-4315

Panama City

2150 Martin Luther King Jr. Blvd.
Panama City Mall #2196
Panama City, FL 32405

Fort Walton Beach

815 Beal Parkway NW
Coastal Bank & Trust Bldg., Suite A
Fort Walton Beach, FL 32547

Pensacola Downtown Greater Pensacola Chamber

117 West Garden Street
Pensacola, FL 32502

Pensacola

9999 University Parkway
Pensacola, Florida 32514-5732

INSTRUCTIONS FOR FLORIDA SUPREME COURT APPROVED FAMILY LAW FORM 12.905(B), SUPPLEMENTAL PETITION FOR MODIFICATION OF CHILD SUPPORT (12/10)

When should this form be used?

This form should be used when you are asking the court to change a current court-ordered child support obligation. The court can change a child support order or judgment if the judge finds that there has been a substantial change in the circumstances of the parties and the change is in the child(ren)'s best interests.

This form should be typed or printed in black ink. After completing this form, you should sign the form before a notary public or deputy clerk. You should file this form in the county where the original order was entered. If the order was entered in another state, or if the child(ren) live(s) in another state, you should speak with an attorney about where to file this form. You should file the original with the clerk of the circuit court and keep a copy for your records.

What should I do next?

For your case to proceed, you must properly notify the other party in your case of the supplemental petition. If you know where he or she lives, you should use personal service.

If you absolutely do not know where he or she lives, you may use constructive service. You may also be able to use constructive service if the other party resides in another state or country. However, if constructive service is used, other than granting a divorce, the court may only grant limited relief.

For more information on constructive service, see Notice of Action for Dissolution of Marriage, Florida Supreme Court Approved Family Law Form 12.913(a), and Affidavit of Diligent Search and Inquiry, Florida Family Law Rules of Procedure Form 12.913(b). If the other party is in the military service of the United States, additional steps for service may be required. See, for example, Memorandum for Certificate of Military Service, Florida Supreme Court Approved Family Law Form 12.912(a). In sum, the law regarding constructive service and service on an individual in the military service is very complex and you may wish to consult an attorney regarding these issues.

If personal service is used, the other party has 20 days to answer after being served with your supplemental petition. Your case will then generally proceed in one of the following three ways:

DEFAULT... If after 20 days, no answer has been filed, you may file a Motion for Default, Florida Supreme Court Approved Family Law Form 12.922(a), with the clerk of court. Then, if you have filed all of the required papers, you may call the clerk, family law intake staff, or judicial assistant to set a final hearing. You must notify the other party of the hearing by using a Notice of Hearing (General), Florida Supreme Court Approved Family Law Form 12.923, or other appropriate notice of hearing form.

UNCONTESTED... If the respondent files an answer that agrees with everything in your supplemental petition or an answer and waiver, and you have complied with mandatory disclosure and filed all of the required papers, you may call the clerk, family law intake staff, or judicial assistant to set a final hearing. You must notify the other party of the hearing by using a Notice of Hearing (General), Florida Supreme Court Approved Family Law Form 12.923, or other appropriate notice of hearing form.

CONTESTED... If the respondent files an answer or an answer and counter petition, which disagrees with or denies anything in your supplemental petition, and you are unable to settle the disputed issues, you should file a Notice for Trial, Florida Supreme Court Approved Family Law Form 12.924, after you have complied with mandatory disclosure and filed all of the required papers. Some circuits may require the completion of mediation before a final hearing may be set. Then you should contact the clerk, family law intake staff, or judicial assistant for instructions on how to set your case for trial (final hearing). If the respondent files an answer and counter petition, you should answer the counter petition within 20 days using an Answer to Counter petition, Florida Supreme Court Approved Family Law Form 12.903(d).

Where can I look for more information?

Before proceeding, you should read "General Information for Self-Represented Litigants" found at the beginning of these forms. The words that are in "bold underline" in these instructions are defined there. For further information, see chapter 61, Florida Statutes.

Special Notes...

If you do not have the money to pay the filing fee, you may obtain an Application for Determination of Civil Indigent Status from the clerk, fill it out, and the clerk will determine whether you are eligible to have filing fees deferred.

With this form, you must also file the following:

Child Support Guidelines Worksheet, Florida Family Law Rules of Procedure Form 12.902(e). (If you do not know the other party's income, you may file this worksheet after his or her financial affidavit has been served on you.) Settlement Agreement, if you have reached an agreement on any or all of the issues. Although there is no form for this in these Florida Family Law Forms, you may construct a settlement agreement using the pertinent sections contained in Marital Settlement Agreement for Dissolution of Marriage with Dependent or Minor Child(ren), Florida Supreme Court Approved Family Law Form 12.902(f)(1). Notice of Social Security Number, Florida Supreme Court Approved Family Law Form 12.902(j), if not previously filed. Family Law Financial Affidavit, Florida Family Law

Rules of Procedure Form 12.902(b) or (c). Certificate of Compliance with Mandatory Disclosure, Florida Family Law Rules of Procedure Form 12.932. (This must be filed within 45 days of service of the supplemental petition on the respondent, if not filed at the time of the supplemental petition, unless you and the other party have agreed not to exchange these documents.)

Child Support... The court may order one parent to pay child support to assist the other parent in meeting the child(ren)'s material needs. Both parents are required to provide financial support, but one parent may be ordered to pay a portion of his or her support for the child(ren) to the other parent. Florida has adopted guidelines for determining the amount of child support to be paid. These guidelines are based on the combined income of both parents and take into account the financial contributions of both parents. You must file a Family Law Financial Affidavit, Florida Family Law Rules of Procedure Form 12.902(b) or (c), and the other parent will be required to do the same. From your financial affidavits, you should be able to calculate the amount of child support that should be paid using the Child Support Guidelines Worksheet, Florida Family Law Rules of Procedure Form 12.902(e). Because the child support guidelines take several factors into consideration, change over time, and vary from state to state, your child support obligation may be more or less than that of other people in seemingly similar situations.

Temporary Relief... If you need temporary relief regarding child support, you may file a Motion for Temporary

Support and Time-Sharing with Dependent or Minor Child(ren), Florida Supreme Court Approved Family Law Form 12.947(a). For more information, see the instructions for that form.

Settlement Agreement... If you and the respondent are able to reach an agreement on any or all of the issues, you should file a Settlement Agreement. Although there is no form for this in these Florida Family Law Forms, you may construct a settlement agreement using the pertinent sections contained in Marital Settlement Agreement for Dissolution of Marriage with Dependent or Minor Child(ren), Florida Supreme Court Approved Family Law Form 12.902(f)(1). Both parties must sign this agreement before a notary public or deputy clerk. Any issues on which you are unable to agree will be considered contested and settled by the judge at the final hearing.

Final Judgment Form... These family law forms contain a Supplemental Final Judgment Modifying Child Support, Florida Supreme Court Approved Family Law Form 12.993(b), which the judge may use. You should check with the clerk, family law intake staff, or judicial assistant to see if you need to bring it with you to the hearing.

If so, you should type or print the heading, including the circuit, county, case number, division, and the parties' names, and leave the rest blank for the judge to complete at your hearing or trial.

Nonlawyer... Remember, a person who is NOT an attorney is called a nonlawyer. If a nonlawyer helps you fill out these forms, that person must give you a copy of a Disclosure from Nonlawyer, Florida Family Law Rules of Procedure Form 12.900(a), before he or she helps you. A nonlawyer helping you fill out these forms also must put his or her name, address, and telephone number on the bottom of the last page of every form he or she helps you complete.

Made in the USA
Coppell, TX
02 December 2020